P9-DNA-627

SELF-DEFENSE: A BASIC COURSE HAS BEEN
ESPECIALLY DEVELOPED FOR THOSE WHO
WANT TO BE ABLE TO TAKE CARE OF THEM-
SELVES WITHOUT SPENDING YEARS IN THE
STUDY OF A MARTIAL ART.

IT IS INTENDED FOR PEOPLE WHO NEED TO
BUILD SELF-CONFIDENCE AND DEVELOP
A FEELING OF COMPETENCE TO COPE WITH
THE THREAT OF PHYSICAL ASSAULT.

THE TECHNIQUES ARE EASY TO LEARN AND
REMEMBER. PREVENTION AND ASSAULT
DETERRENCE ARE EMPHASIZED.

TEGNER PRESENTS NEW, HUMANISTIC VIEWS
OF THE MASCULINE ROLE AS IT RELATES TO
VIOLENCE, SELF-RESPECT AND SELF-DEFENSE.

BOOKS BY BRUCE TEGNER

BRUCE TEGNER'S COMPLETE BOOK of SELF-DEFENSE

BRUCE TEGNER'S COMPLETE BOOK of KARATE

BRUCE TEGNER'S COMPLETE BOOK of JUDO

BRUCE TEGNER'S COMPLETE BOOK of AIKIDO

BRUCE TEGNER'S COMPLETE BOOK of JUKADO

BRUCE TEGNER'S COMPLETE BOOK of JUJITSU

SELF-DEFENSE: A BASIC COURSE

SELF-DEFENSE for YOUR CHILD (With Alice McGrath)
    Elementary school age boys & girls

SELF-DEFENSE for BOYS & MEN: A Physical Education Course

SELF-DEFENSE and ASSAULT PREVENTION for
    GIRLS & WOMEN (With Alice McGrath)

SELF-DEFENSE NERVE CENTERS & PRESSURE POINTS

KARATE: Self-Defense & Traditional Sport Forms

KARATE & JUDO EXERCISES

STICK-FIGHTING: SPORT FORMS

STICK-FIGHTING: SELF-DEFENSE

BLACK BELT JUDO, KARATE, JUKADO

AIKIDO and Jiu Jitsu Holds & Locks

SAVATE: French Foot & Fist Fighting

JUDO: Sport Techniques for Physical Fitness & Tournament

DEFENSE TACTICS for LAW ENFORCEMENT:
    Weaponless Defense & Control and Baton Techniques

KUNG FU & TAI CHI: Chinese Karate & Classical Exercise

Additional titles in preparation

SELF-DEFENSE:
A BASIC COURSE
BRUCE TEGNER

THOR PUBLISHING CO.   VENTURA CA. 93001

Library of Congress Cataloging in Publication Data

Tegner, Bruce.
  Self-defense, a basic course.

  Includes index.
  1. Self-defense. I. Title.
GV111.T43   796.8'1   79-13556
ISBN 0-87407-517-3
ISBN 0-87407-031-7 pbk.

Selection and organization of the defense techniques and the
introductory material in this book are new. The photos were
taken from Bruce Tegner's Complete Book of Self-Defense.

SELF-DEFENSE: A BASIC COURSE
First printing: May 1979

SELF-DEFENSE: A BASIC COURSE
Copyright © 1979 by Bruce Tegner & Alice McGrath
All rights reserved. This book may not be reproduced in
whole or in part without the written permission of the
publisher.

THOR PUBLISHING COMPANY
P. O. BOX 1782
VENTURA, CA 93001   *Printed in U.S.A.*

BRUCE TEGNER'S COMPLETE BOOK OF SELF-DEFENSE
Recommended for Y.A. in the American Library Association
BOOKLIST

BRUCE TEGNER'S COMPLETE BOOK OF JUDO
"...the definitive text...ideal for instructors and individuals."
SCHOLASTIC COACH

BRUCE TEGNER'S COMPLETE BOOK OF JUJITSU
"...authoritative and easy-to-follow text...clear photos."
SCHOOL LIBRARY JOURNAL

KARATE: Self-defense & Traditional Forms
Recommended for Y.A. in the American Library Association
BOOKLIST

BRUCE TEGNER'S COMPLETE BOOK OF KARATE
"Tegner suggests and illustrates changes to bring karate in
line with modern concepts of physical education...invaluable
for teaching karate in schools, colleges and recreation centers."
CAPHER

SELF-DEFENSE FOR YOUR CHILD (with Alice McGrath)
[For elementary school age boys & girls]
"...informative, readable book for family use..."
CHRISTIAN HOME & SCHOOL

"...intelligent, clear-headed approach..."   BOOKS WEST

SELF-DEFENSE & ASSAULT PREVENTION FOR GIRLS & WOMEN (with
Alice McGrath)
"...should be required reading for all girls and women..."
WILSON LIBRARY BULLETIN
"...simple and straightforward with no condescension...easy to
learn and viable as defense tactics..."   SCHOOL LIBRARY JOURNAL

BRUCE TEGNER'S COMPLETE BOOK OF JUKADO
"This is the most useful book on the Oriental fighting arts I
have ever seen."   LIBRARY JOURNAL

SELF-DEFENSE NERVE CENTERS & PRESSURE POINTS
"Students and teachers will find much valuable source
material in this attractive book."   SCHOLASTIC COACH

SELF-DEFENSE FOR BOYS & MEN: A Physical Education Course
"...recommended for school libraries. The text deserves
inspection by P.E. instructors."   LIBRARY JOURNAL

KUNG FU & TAI CHI: Chinese Karate and Classical Exercise
"...recommended for physical fitness collections."
LIBRARY JOURNAL

THE AUTHOR THANKS

RAY COLEMAN
ROCKY ESCALANTI
JEFF HAGER
DON HAIRSTON
KELLY McENROE
RICHARD WINDISHAR

for demonstrating the techniques in the photos.

CONTENTS

NEW CONCEPTS OF SELF-DEFENSE/11
RANGE OF RESPONSES/11
LEVEL OF SKILL/12
MASCULINE MYTH/13
TV, MOVIES & THE IMAGE/14
IDENTIFICATION/15
PASSIVITY IS DANGEROUS/16
WINNERS & LOSERS/16
BODY IMAGE & SELF-ESTEEM/17
PHYSICAL ACTIVITY/17
GENERAL COMPETENCE/18
GUNS FOR SELF-DEFENSE/19
FIGHTING IN FILMS/20
AVOIDANCE/21
HITCHHIKING/21
DEFENSES DON'T WORK AGAINST FRIENDS/22
HOW TO USE THE BOOK/23
SAFETY IN PRACTICE/23
TAPPING FOR SAFETY/24
WORK SLOWLY/25
WORKING WITH A PARTNER/25
HAND CONDITIONING: A WARNING/26
HAND BLOWS/27
EDGE-OF-THE-HAND CHOP/27
HOW TO STRIKE/30
CLOSE-IN TARGET AREAS/31
EFFECTS OF THE BLOWS/33
HEEL-OF-PALM BLOW/34
POKING/34

HAMMER BLOW/35
FIST BLOWS/36
ELBOW BLOW/37
KICKING FOR SELF-DEFENSE/37
PRACTICAL KICKS/40
STAMP KICK/41
SNAP KICK/43
BLOCK & PARRY/44
SLAPPING PARRY/45
SLASHING PARRY/46
RESPONSE TO FRONT REACH/48
BLOCKING THE FOUR QUARTERS/50
GESTURES OF ASSERTION/52
THE JOLLY BULLY/55
THE HAND SQUEEZER/56
THE LEANER/58
THE SHOULDER PUNCHER/BACK SLAPPER/59
BEAR HUG/60
BUTT GRIP/62
FIGHTING STANCES: PRO & CON/63
READY STANCES/63
QUICK RESPONSE TO BACK THREAT/66
DISTRACTION/69
FEINTING DISTRACTIONS/69
SPIN AROUNDS/71
ARM SPIN-AROUND/71
BODY SPIN-AROUND/72
JUDO THROWS/73
TAKEDOWNS/74
FOREWARD TAKEDOWN/74
BACK TAKEDOWN/75
HOLDS & LOCKS FOR RESTRAINT/76
BASIC ARM BAR/76
REAR BENT-ARM LOCK/78
COMPLETE DEFENSES/80
ON-GOING DEFENSE/80
FLEXIBLE COMBINATIONS/80
COMPLETE COMBINATIONS/81

YELLING AS A DEFENSE AID/83
FULL-NELSON RELEASE/84
HEADLOCK RELEASES/86
FOREARM CHOKE: MUGGING DEFENSE/88
DEFENSES AGAINST KICKING ASSAULTS/91
TOE KICK/KNEE KICK/91
PIN ESCAPE/93
RIGID WEAPON ASSAULTS/94
OUTSIDE SWING/94
BACK-HANDED SWING/95
FLEXIBLE WEAPONS/96
YOKING ARM PIN RELEASE/98
KNIFE ASSAULT DEFENSE/102
CLOSE-IN KNIFE THREAT/102
AFTERWORD/105
FURTHER STUDY/105
CHOOSING A SCHOOL/106
DOES TEACHER NEED A BLACK BELT?/107
COLORED BELTS/108
INDEX/110

We need a new concept of masculinity; one based on the idea of responsibility and care for others, rather than upon a disregard of physical dangers which so often recoils, not only upon the man intent on proving his manhood, but upon others who die as the result of his recklessness.

—ANTHONY STORR

NEW CONCEPTS OF SELF-DEFENSE

The techniques in this book have been selected after many years of teaching and research in the field. They are techniques which most people are able to learn with relative ease. They are techniques which most people can learn and remember without constant practice.

Although the defenses are based on ancient jujitsu there are three fundamental differences between this new method of self-defense and the procedures and concepts which are characteristic of old-style martial arts.

In traditional martial arts every assault is treated as if it were a serious or deadly attack. Most defenses are taught as specific reactions to specific attacks. A high level of skill is the objective of training in martial arts specialties such as karate, aikido and jujitsu.

RANGE OF RESPONSES

In my view, the basis for a rational, ethical, practical method of self-defense is the recognition that there is a wide range of aggressive actions from mildly hostile to very serious. Defense actions should be appropriate to the situation. Treating all aggressive actions as though they were vicious assault is counterproductive. Individuals who are taught to defend themselves against a serious assault but do not know how to cope with demeaning horseplay have the choice of overreacting or not reacting at all. Overreacting means using more force than is appropriate. Passive submission may result in persistent feelings of powerlessness, rage, frustration and humiliation. Such feelings lead to a loss of self-respect and self-control.

LEVEL OF SKILL

Because traditional methods of self-defense are based on
the assumption that students will spend years in learning
and practicing, the techniques which are taught are complicated and difficult and all students are expected to
achieve a high level of skill. The teaching methods are
geared to the very able. Those who do not have superior
athletic ability or who are not committed to long-range
programs of training and practice are neglected, or drop out.

A high degree of proficiency is neither necessary nor
possible to achieve in a basic course.

Most of the defense actions are effective even when they
are applied with a moderate degree of skill. Develop the
highest level of skill that you can, but remember that this
course was developed to be used by ordinary people, not
highly trained experts, and that you do not need more than
functional skill.

A feature of many of the martial arts training programs
is contest or contest-like practice procedures. In many of
the schools which follow traditional methods, contest
training is given to all students, regardless of their needs
or abilities.

Learning basic self-defense is like learning basic swimming
skills. To become a champion swimmer you would have
to devote years to training and practice. To learn functional
swimming requires relatively little time and practice. Competition in any sport demands brilliant technique and vir-
tuoso performance. Practical skills require only functional
ability. You do not need championship fighting ability to
learn and use practical self-defense.

Instead of learning rigid routines of attack/defense, this
method presents you with a small group of defense actions
which can be used in flexible combinations. As you will
see, it is possible to learn defenses against common types
of assault without having to memorize series of "moves"
to be performed in an exact order.

MASCULINE MYTH

Almost anyone can learn self-defense in a relatively short time without becoming a skilled fighter. The major obstacle to learning and teaching self-defense to young men is the persistence of a myth about self-defense and masculinity. The myth, still widely believed, is that the ability to defend against physical assault is a built-in masculine trait. Masculinity is equated with an innate ability to win fights and to inflict physical punishment.

The myth of inborn masculine aggressiveness is the opposite and supporting myth of inherent feminine helplessness and passivity.

The ability to defend against assault is neither a masculine nor a feminine trait--it is a learned skill. Self-defense is not an instinctive, automatic male response. If it were, then all males could defend themselves and no females would be able to learn self-defense.

Every culture has its own definition of what constitutes correct male behavior. These expectations and definitions for male (and female) behavior are different in different parts of the world and in different times. These differences have produced a wide range of behavior among men and women throughout the world and throughout recorded history. Men are questioning the role that is assigned to them according to the current definition of manliness, just as women are rejecting the notion that they are inferior to men. Both men and women are born with the potential to acquire skills that have nothing to do with femininity or masculinity.

TV, MOVIES & THE IMAGE

The image of males as inherently violent and aggressive
is powerfully projected on television and movie screens.

On television and in movie theaters there is constant
reinforcement of the myth that manly men are violent.
The message coming from the screens is that there are only
two kinds of men--the dominating, violent, punishing,
vigilante male who is admired, and the passive, helpless,
incompetent victim who is despised or pitied.

Since neither of these stereotypes offers a satisfying
model for self-actualization in the real world it appears
that there are two intolerable alternatives and no acceptable
choices.

A REAL CHOICE

The either/or fallacy has been accepted for such a long time
and reinforced with such persistence that it is widely
believed that there are only two roles available--the aggressor
or the victim. It is widely believed that the alternative to
becoming a highly trained fighter is to be a helpless person
unable to cope with the threat of assault. The choice seems
to be between passivity or aggression.

There is another choice but it is seldom portrayed on the
screen and not often discussed. The rational alternative
to aggression is not submission, but assertion. The rational
choice is to refuse to play the game of abused-or-abuser.
The life-enhancing choice is to become self-reliant, able to
cope with the threat of assault using the least possible force
and knowing the procedures which minimize the possibility
of having to use physical defense actions.

IDENTIFICATION

Entertainment violence is a distorted reflection of violence
on the street and in the home. There is plenty of violence
in the real world; television and movie violence is glamorized
and glorified, dramatized and exaggerated.

Those who regularly watch many hours of television every
day and see a disproportionate amount of violence in
relation to other human activities tend to overestimate
the danger of assault. They become confused about the
circumstances in which the danger of violence is a reality.

Television watchers and the fans of "action" films ("action"
is the public relations code word for violence) tend to
identify with extremes of behavior. Some identify with
highly aggressive punitive behavior and some with extremely
passive behavior.

Those who identify with the super-hero vigilante-avenger
accept violence as an appropriate reaction to any event
which threatens or disturbs them.

Those who identify with the victims of violence or the
passive bystanders tend to become passive in real life
and underestimate their ability to cope with common
everyday problems.

There is accumulating evidence that those who identify
with punitive, violent behavior are more likely to become
violent under stress.

There is incontrovertible evidence that those who submit
passively to aggression or threat of violence are more
likely to be hurt than those who make an orderly show of
resistance or take avoidance measures.

PASSIVITY IS DANGEROUS

Resisting does not necessarily mean hitting or physical
confrontation. Resistance may take the form of verbal
responses to cool down the situation. Resistance may
take the form of mild physical actions which convey the
message that you intend to avoid the role of helpless victim.
Resistance might be communicated by body gesture and
facial expression which expresses assertiveness without
being challenging. Resistance might take the form of
spirited, forceful use of defense actions if no other option
is available.

New students are likely to express the worry that if they
resist assault they will be hurt more than if they submit.
Real life experiences and studies done by professionals
in the field of law enforcement and psychology support
the view that resistance to unarmed assault is much safer
than passive submission.

WINNERS & LOSERS

Assault is not a sporting event. Self-defense should not be
classified with or confused with sport or contest. Partici-
pants in a sport contest have agreed to compete. They are
bound by a set of predetermined rules which apply to
both contestants equally.

Contestants in a sporting event are matched according to
level of skill. In most sports activities there are safeguards
against injury and any deliberate effort to cause injury is
a foul. The objective of a sport contest is to win!

There are no referees and no rules of sportsmanship in
an assault. "Winning" is an irrelevant concept for basic
self-defense. Escape or avoidance would be first choice
responses. Successful resistance to assault does not mean
winning a fight; it means demonstrating determination to
avoid the role of docile, passive victim!

There are no winners in an assault. Both the assailant
and the victim are losers. The victim loses self-respect.
The assailant loses self-control.

BODY IMAGE & SELF-ESTEEM

Many people who feel vulnerable to assault expose their vulnerability through behavior and in their physical appearance and demeanor. Obsessive fear of assault or the feeling of incompetence to deal with the threat of assault diminishes self-esteem.

My view of self-defense training differs from the traditional in that I do not accept the premise that competitive activities are necessarily appropriate or useful for people who need to improve body image and self-esteem.

When there is a lack of self-esteem it shows in facial expression, in docile behavior, and in general lack of confidence.

When there is a poor body image it shows in posture, movement and gait.

PHYSICAL ACTIVITY

Body image can be improved in many instances through a program of acquiring body skills. My experience suggests that those who benefit to the greatest degree from self-defense instruction are those least likely to have the interest, inclination or aptitude to perform well in body-contact or competitive sports. They do better and benefit more from solo or non-competitive activities.

Swimming, running, bicycling, calisthenics, dancing, yoga, moderate weight training, gymnastics, tai chi and other such solo activities can improve your health, coordination, posture, appearance and body image without having to be compared with the abilities of other people. You do not need an opponent in order to measure your progress. You can measure progress in relation to your own starting point.

The physical program you choose should suit your interest, your inclination, your present level of physical ability and your temperament.

Solo and noncompetitive physical activities--and those in which competition is secondary to the pleasure of playing-- are likely to become life-long recreation, thus offering greater opportunity for continuing development of mental and physical health.

Regular physical activity is a release for mental and emotional stress. It will make you feel better inside and outside.

GENERAL COMPETENCE

Self-esteem can be acquired. Becoming self-confident is not an event; it is a process. Learning self-defense can be a step in the direction of developing your sense of self-reliance and self-confidence.

But any other activity or skill that you acquire can also enhance your feeling of self-worth and self-respect. Along with your self-defense training program you might benefit greatly from a program of general self-improvement which could include education, technical skills, on the job training for advancement, or participation in assertiveness training.

If you are still in school, take your education seriously and push for excellence. It will pay off in self-regard, self-confidence and sense of self-worth.

If you have dropped out or are past public school age, find the free, low-cost or subsidized programs of instruction and group activity in your community. Adult education, job training programs, recreation centers and Ys have a wide range of appropriate classes.

The more you develop your potential abilities into skills and activities the better you will feel about yourself. The better you feel about yourself the better you will feel about other people. When you feel better about yourself, other people will react to your self-regard by respecting you.

MORE SELF-DEFENSE

Among those who start self-defense at the basic level, there will be some who might wish to continue into a specialty of the martial arts. See pages 105-108 for some advice and comments.

GUNS FOR SELF-DEFENSE?

In my view, there are practical, ethical and psychological arguments against owning handguns for self-defense which far outweigh any possible advantage.

There are some special instances, professionals in law enforcement and individuals living in remote, isolated areas, for instance, in which guns might be an appropriate protection. But my reasons and arguments apply to the general public--to the person who has or is considering owning a gun for personal defense.

A gun or any other weapon is not adequate protection unless it is carried at all times. The alternative to carrying it on your person at all times is to have it easily accessible to you at all times. If it is easily accessible to you, it is easily accessible to others, including children.

A study in the Cleveland, Ohio area revealed that householders who armed themselves to protect their homes, shot and killed seventeen intruders in a fourteen-year period. During that same period in the same area, 102 family members, friends and neighbors were killed by handguns. For each intruder shot and killed, gun owners killed six innocent people - including their own children, wives, husbands, parents and neighbors.

FIGHTING IN FILMS

Every fight scene in a movie is planned, move by move, blow
by blow. Whether or not the actors in TV shows and films
have any fighting skill is irrelevant. Fight scenes are played
by actors who are paid to act the roles of villains and the
roles of heroes. The heroes do not win movie fights because
they can fight better than the villains, but because the script
tells them when to win and when to lose. Even when actors
have fighting skill, the story determines what they are going
to do and how to do it.

Films and TV shows are not made to instruct us but to
amaze and entertain us. Off-stage trampolines are used so
that actors can leap higher than any human could in
real life. Stunt men are paid to tumble and fall in a way
that makes it appear they have sustained forceful blows.
Villains carefully stay out of the way of the hero until it is
their turn to be chopped, stabbed or leaped at.

In my experience working in films, I have often had the job
of training the hero to play a fight scene which I have de-
signed; then I have worked with stunt men, coaching them
to lose the fight in the most spectacular manner; then I have
played the role of a villain, "losing" the fight to the hero
whom I had taught to "win" the fight.

Rick Nelson and James Coburn are among the actors I
have worked with whose ability to learn and perform in
fight scenes is really outstanding. Nevertheless, in the films
where these skills were used, the fight scene itself was carefully planned, rehearsed over and over, and filmed according
to the script. This is what makes film fighting different from
a street defense.

In the movies, if the actor performs the dazzling and difficult
fighting technique less than perfectly, they shoot the scene
over. So no matter what style of fighting is shown or the
circumstances of the fight scene, the hero wins when he
ought to and loses when the plot reads that way. This
explains why the style of fighting in the movies is of no
particular value as a guide to practical self-defense.

AVOIDANCE

Men are far more likely to be the victims of assault than are women. Women are encouraged to avoid high-risk-of-assault situations, but men are rarely advised to do so, even though the risk for men is greater than that for women.

At any public gathering where people might get excited or angry it is prudent to be alert to signs of impending violence. If you leave before emotions get out of hand, it is much safer than if you wait until fighting starts.

At parties it is relatively easy to determine that a fight is likely to start. Verbal hostility usually precedes physical violence. Challenging, hostile behavior should be your cue to leave as quickly and as quietly as possible.

RUN AWAY

Running away is a prudent and sensible response to the threat of physical violence. Whenever and wherever you can escape threatened assault by running away, you should do it! There is no "honor" in an assault and there is no loss of honor if you run away.

HITCHHIKING

Hitchhiking involves a high risk of assault. The assailant might be the hitchhiker or the driver. In either case, you must make an *immediate* response to any behavior that makes you uncomfortable or wary.

If you have picked up someone or have been picked up by someone whose conversation or actions make you feel that you are in a vulnerable situation you must react promptly. If you are the hitchhiker, tell the driver to stop and let you out. If you are assertive and positive, there is little chance that the driver will refuse. Assailants, especially in this kind of situation, are looking for easy victims.

If you are the driver, stop the car at the first possible opportunity and command the hitchhiker to get out.

In either case if the object is robbery and if the person
is armed, it is most prudent not to resist.

If you are driving alone and someone is hitchhiking at
what appears to be a stranded vehicle, you do not have to
stop in order to give the person help. Make a mental note
of the location and the color and make of the car. Stop at
the nearest highway emergency phone or at the next gas
station and report the trouble.

DEFENSES DON'T WORK AGAINST FRIENDS

The defenses you will practice in this course have been
selected for practicality and effectiveness. Testing them
on friends is not valid. You can learn them with a friend,
but you cannot prove them against a friend.

To prove the effectiveness of a technique you would have
to apply it realistically. Obviously you cannot do that with
techniques which result in considerable pain. For instance,
you know that a forceful kick into the shin causes a great
deal of pain. In practice with your friend, you merely
simulate the action and acknowledge the fact that it would
work for street defense.

The result of trying to "prove" self-defense to friends and
acquaintances is disappointing and negative. If you did the
defense vigorously and with spirit, it would be effective.
Simulating the defense is perfectly appropriate for learning
self-defense, but not a very satisfactory way of "proving"
that you can defend yourself.

The element of surprise works for you in self-defense. Even
in a friendly game you do not alert your opponent to your
plans. In self-defense you would not tell your adversary
what you plan to do. In demonstrating the effectiveness
of the techniques to friends, you lose the advantage of
surprise and you cannot make full-power contact blows.
Self-defense is not a game. It is meant for and works in
emergency situations--when you need it!

HOW TO USE THE BOOK

If you are learning self-defense at home or with a group which does not have teacher supervision, follow these procedures:

Before you practice the defenses, read all of the introductory material carefully. Give a quick reading to the instruction text to become familiar with the scope of the material and the concepts on which the course is based. Glance at the photos to become familiar with gesture and movement.

Pay special attention to information about safety in practice.

The simplest way to use the book for home study is to practice the actions in the same order as they appear in the book.

For each technique, follow this procedure: First reread the text carefully and compare the written description with the photo illustration. You should understand the essential movement and the application of the technique before you practice it.

When you feel that you have grasped the fundamental mechanics of the technique and can perform it without gross error, move on to the next technique.

SAFETY IN PRACTICE

There is no need for either partner to be hurt during practice of self-defense techniques.

The techniques in this course have been selected after many years of teaching experience and research. They are effective! It is not the aim of this course to *prove* to you that they work; it is the purpose of this course to *teach* you the techniques. Working carefully and correctly will give you better preparation for defense than working in a rough style. Observe the safety advice and comply with the instructions.

Although the text is written as though you were using the
defense actions against an assailant, you *simulate* the techniques with your partner.

Use your imagination. You know that if you were kicked
vigorously in the shin you would feel considerable pain. But
when you are practicing how to kick into the shin, you
simulate the action. You do not really kick your partner
in the shin. Your gesture, your expression, your body and
leg movement can be realistically forceful--but you are
careful not to make contact.

When you are learning the ways of hitting and kicking, you
may touch your partner *very lightly*, just to feel the proper
position and relationship.

In any kind of body-contact physical activity a prime rule
of safety in practice is: DON'T FOOL AROUND!! Self-
defense is not a game; it is a serious, practical skill.

TAPPING FOR SAFETY

Tapping is the signal for "stop" in the practice of these
techniques. The three ways of stopping the action are
tapping the floor, your partner, or yourself.

Tap when you feel pain. Tap when a technique is applied
correctly and you want to tell your partner "that is enough."
Tap if your partner works in a rough or incorrect manner.
Tap when your partner is making an obvious error and you
want to correct him.

IMMEDIATELY upon feeling or hearing the tapping
signal from your partner, you must stop! If you work with
a partner who ignores the tapping signal or who consistently
works in a rough manner, you should ask for a different
partner. It is not brave, it is foolish to work with a partner
who ignores the safety rules.

WORK SLOWLY

Working slowly is a precautionary procedure and a good learning method. It is more important to learn the correct gesture and action of the defense techniques than it is to move fast. Particularly in the beginning, you will learn better if you pace your actions to your ability.

A technique which you learn properly can be speeded up as you progress. Speed of execution, in any case, is not as important as you might think.

Self-defense is a life-long skill. As a life-long skill it is more important that you perform the defense actions with spirit, an appearance of determination and an inner conviction of self-reliance.

Working slowly, you can concentrate on the essential elements of practical self-defense. You can learn the correct actions and you can rehearse the appropriate responses.

WORKING WITH A PARTNER

You can become familiar with self-defense and even learn minimum techniques by reading the book and going through the defenses and techniques by yourself, but obviously that is not the best way to practice.

The ideal partner is someone who has the same degree of interest that you have and who will work through the course with you on an equal basis.

If you have a group of three, you can take turns practicing in rotation, with the third person given the assignment of reading the instruction and watching for mistakes. If you have a group of four, change partners from session to session.

HAND CONDITIONING: A WARNING

There is no need to condition your hands for either sport
or self-defense fighting skills. Hand conditioning is a process of hardening and desensitizing the hands. Individuals
with heavily conditioned hands can do sensational breaking
tricks and they can hit hard surfaces with full-power blows
without hurting themselves, for they have lost the ability
to feel pain.

The process of hand conditioning had a function in the
past. When karate fighters had to break through wooden
armor, they needed to make weapons of their hands. When
karate was intended for hand-to-hand combat with the objective of killing the enemy, karate fighters had to spend
years to prepare for battle.

Extreme hand conditioning can seriously impair manual
dexterity and the disability is permanent. Once you lose
the ability to do intricate, delicate movements with your
hands because of extreme hand conditioning, you cannot
regain it.

For self-defense, conditioned hands could be an impediment
rather than an asset. If self-defense is viewed (as I view it) as
preparation to avoid fighting and to use the least amount of
force if one has to fight, how is it possible to reconcile
heavily conditioned hands with that objective? If one gives
the appearance of preparing to fight by conditioning the
hands, it is difficult to maintain the role of self-defender;
conditioned hands give the appearance of preparation for
aggression.

Since the great majority of you reading my books are young
people, I would particularly warn you against hand conditioning. The youthful indiscretion of hand conditioning
can be regretted, but it cannot be undone.

HAND BLOWS

Practical hand blows for self-defense are those which the average person can use without having years of training and without engaging in constant practice to maintain proficiency.

The types of hand blows should be appropriate for use in a range of situations from annoying to moderately serious to vicious assault. A mildly annoying situation should not be treated as though it were serious assault. The appropriate response to a vicious assault is different from the response to a humiliating, but not dangerous, aggressive action.

For practical, basic self-defense I have selected only those hand blows which most people can learn and use with relative ease. I have eliminated those which are effective only if they are used by a highly trained expert.

The hand blows can be used in a manner ranging from mildly deterrent, through moderately vigorous, to forceful.

EDGE-OF-THE-HAND: THE CHOP

Hitting with the side of the hand, along the outside edge, is an efficient self-defense technique.

Using this open-hand blow you can hit or parry without coming into fist-hitting range of an assailant. Another advantage of this blow is that you should be able to strike full-force without hurting yourself. If you hit correctly you can deliver a forceful blow without danger of injury to your hand.

To determine the exact striking area, hit lightly onto a hard surface, such as a table top, positioning your hand to avoid striking with the bony parts. Your hand should be slightly cupped and slightly tilted so that you hit with the fleshy edge of your palm.

1   2

If your hand is tilted back too far you will hit the wrist
bone. If it is tilted too far forward you will hit the little
finger bone. Adjust the position of your hand until you
feel comfortable striking a moderate blow onto the hard
surface.

The edge-of-hand blow is commonly called a "chop" or
"slash." It is delivered with a quick, snappy action.

Arm targets you can hit, without getting within striking
distance of your adversary's hand, are: wrist, forearm, and
into the bend of the elbow.

1. Hit at the wrist with a snappy, choppy action to divert
the intended blow downward . . .

2. . . . or outward.

3   4

3. If you extend your arm fully, palm down, you will see a pronounced mound on your forearm just beyond your elbow. At this mound there is a vulnerable area which can be struck with the edge-of-hand blow . . .

4. . . . using either hand for striking.

Hitting at the wrist can divert an intended blow. Hitting onto the mound of the forearm results in pain. If the blow is struck with force, it can numb the arm briefly.

We are so conditioned to move in closer to an adversary in order to deal with him that it takes conscious effort and practice to overcome the habit. Step *away* from your adversary whenever it is appropriate and possible. If you come in close to hit him, you are placing yourself in hitting range.

HOW TO STRIKE

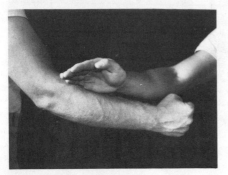

5

This close-up shows the correct position for the open-hand slash/chop. Note that the hand is slightly cupped and the striking point is at the fleshy part of the palm.

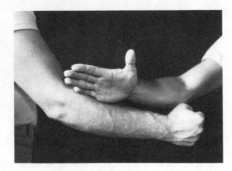

6. *Avoid this error.*

Do not hold your thumb up; it should be held as in photo 5. Holding your thumb up decreases efficiency.

7   8

CLOSE-IN TARGET AREAS

Hitting at targets which can only be reached close in, putting you within the assailant's hitting range, should be reserved for those situations in which you are already close and cannot move away, or when it is appropriate to the circumstance. In the event of serious assault you would not, by choice, step in close to the assailant if you could avoid it.

7. Strike palm up with the edge of your hand, into the side of the neck.

8. Or strike into the side of the neck back-handed, palm down.

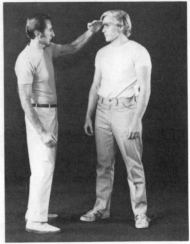

9   10

9. Or use both hands to strike into both sides of the neck with simultaneous blows.

10. Strike sharply onto the bridge of the nose.

11. Use a back-handed slash up under the nose.

12. Hitting at an assailant behind you, the chop can be used to hit downward onto a reaching arm . . .

11   12

13

13. . . . or back-handed into the side of the neck.

EFFECTS OF THE BLOWS

Striking the side of the neck is an excellent self-defense tactic and does not involve a high risk of injury. Although striking into the side of the neck could cause considerable pain and perhaps briefly stun the assailant, it is unlikely that a smaller person defending against a larger assailant could deliver a hand blow with enough force to cause unconsciousness.

Hitting onto the nose causes pain and disorientation.

Hitting up under the nose also causes pain and disorientation, but it is not, as is widely believed, a deadly blow which could drive nasal bones into the brain. The only skull opening above the nose is a tiny aperture. The nasal bones would have to be pulverized in order to enter through it. The notion that hitting up under the nose is a fatal blow derives from an ignorance of anatomy.

A very forceful blow struck anywhere into the head involves
a danger of serious injury. The effect of any blow to the
head is a function of impact force. It does not matter what
type of blow is used or where the blow lands; if great force
is used to hit into the head, injury or fatality may result.

HEEL-OF-PALM BLOW

14. Curl your fingers back and hit with the fleshy part of
the base of your palm.

The heel-of-palm blow can be delivered as a moderate,
pushing action, or if appropriate, it can be delivered as a
forceful, upward smashing blow.

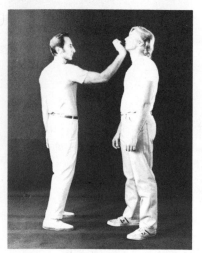
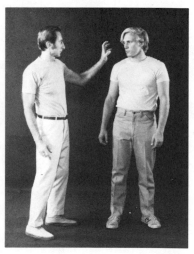

14   15

POKING

15. The claw-like poking blow can be used as a distraction
by thrusting your hand *toward* the assailant's face, or it can
be used as a blow which is completed by hitting his face with
the palm of your hand. In the event of serious, dangerous
assault, it can be used as a blow into the eyes. Hitting into
the eyes is a high-risk-of-injury blow. It is appropriate only
if the assault is vicious and cannot be stopped with less
risk of injury.

Partners must be particularly careful in practice of the
poking technique; slight contact involves possibility of eye
injury. The distance shown in the photo is close enough
for simulation practice.

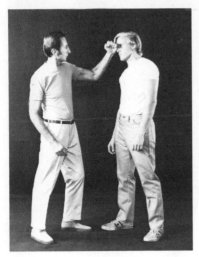 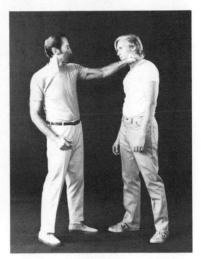

16   17

HAMMER BLOW

16. A hammer blow struck with the edge of the closed
fist has limited application, but it is a useful self-defense
tactic close in. You can strike down onto the nose . . .

17. . . . or into the side of the neck.

Hitting at bony targets, the clavicle for instance, is more
appropriate for movie fights than it is for real people.
Hitting at a bony target has one of two effects--either nothing
happens, or bones are broken. To break bones, a high degree
of skill and force is required. For practical self-defense,
learning to break bones with a hammer blow is unnecessary.

18   19

FIST BLOWS

If you feel comfortable with and can use standard boxing
fist blows, there is no need to change your style. You can
add variety and versatility by incorporating the foregoing
hand blows, but you need not discard boxing blows if you
can use them efficiently.

The karate fist blow is delivered with the two large knuckles.
An upward karate fist blow resembles the standard boxing
upper-cut.

18. Using traditional boxing fist blows or karate-style
punching, select a target area more suitable for defense than
the head or face. The mid-body can be struck with less
force than is needed to hit into bony, protected body target
areas. You can strike straight in . . .

19. . . . or hit in an upward direction.

20   21

ELBOW BLOW

20. The point of the elbow can be used to deliver a blow back into the mid-section, or . . .

21. . . . into the side of the head, neck or face.

KICKING FOR SELF-DEFENSE

In the United States, there is a general aversion to kicking. We think that bad guys kick, but that good guys do not. Assailants kick, but their victims, by some odd kind of reasoning, are prohibited from kicking in self-defense because kicking is "dirty" fighting.

There is no "fair" assault. Techniques, in themselves, are neither fair nor unfair. The total situation, including techniques, has to be evaluated.

Fist blows, which would be "fair" in one kind of situation, would be grossly unfair in another. If two individuals of approximately the same size, weight and skill enter willingly into a match and both use fist blows, fist blows are fair. If a strong, heavy individual assaults a small frail person with fist blows, fist blows are unfair.

22

In a match in which foot blows are forbidden, kicking is
clearly unfair.

Using kicks in self-defense against an assailant is neither
fair nor unfair, since the concept of fairness doesn't apply.

22. The men shown here are about equal in size, weight
and reach. In a sport they would be well matched. They
could engage in a fair contest by following the rules of
that contest.

Consider a different situation. The man on the right is
threatening assault; the man on the left does not want to
fight.

If the belligerent person insists on fighting, the defense
should be as efficient as possible and on terms which give
the defending individual the best chance of stopping the
assault without getting hurt.

23

23. Rather than moving in to use his hands, thereby putting himself within hitting range of his assailant, a more effective defense action is to move back out of range of his adversary's reach . . .

24

24. . . . ready to kick, if it is necessary.

Avoid thinking in terms of sporting matches or combat. For
practical self-defense, choose the most effective techniques
and use the least possible force. If foot blows are appropriate, use them.

When the assailant is larger and stronger than the intended
victim, the smaller person is at a considerable disadvantage
using hand blows. Using kicks, a smaller person can stop an
intended assault and make an orderly defense.

In addition to keeping you out of fist range of your assailant,
kicks offer other advantages. Your leg is stronger than your
arm, so you can deliver a more powerful blow with your
foot than with your hand. Though street fighters use kicks,
they do not expect their intended victims to kick. You have
the element of surprise in your favor when you kick for
defense.

PRACTICAL KICKS

The spectacular high kicks taught in traditional karate and
savate have no practical application for self-defense. These
high, difficult kicks are for contest, and are learned only
with considerable effort and continuing practice.

The kicks adapted here for self-defense are modified versions
of karate and savate kicking. They are aimed at low body
targets and they can be learned by most people with relative
ease. These kicks can be used with moderate force, when
appropriate, and with considerable power when necessary.

25

STAMP KICK

25. Using the bottom of your foot or shoe, deliver a stamping kick forward . . .

26. . . . or to the rear.

26

27

27. Kick into the back of the knee to put an assailant off balance. A vigorous kick could put him on the ground.

A stamp kick can be used onto the instep (shown in photo 30).

In practice with your partner, you must always observe the safety rules. After you learn the correct gesture and delivery of the kicks in solo practice, you may practice with your partner *without* making contact. Some photos illustrate how the kicks would be applied in defense use, but for practice you need not get any closer than shown in photo 25. You can simulate the kicks with realistic vigor if you are careful to avoid contact.

SNAP KICK

28. The outside edge of your foot or shoe can deliver a
snappy kick of moderate or considerable force, depending on
the circumstance. The entire length of the edge of your shoe
is the striking area; this positioning ensures that you can hit
the target without having to practice for precise accuracy.

The snap kick can be directed low on the shin, or into the
mid-shin. Anywhere along the shin, from just below the knee
down to the ankle, is a suitable target. You can kick into the
ankle as well.

The edge-of-shoe snap kick is delivered fairly close in for
practical defense. The action is sharp and snappy.

29. You can snap-kick to the rear without having to turn
around or shift foot position. Kick into the shin . . .

28   29

30

30. . . . and follow through by scraping down the shin with the edge of your shoe. Complete the action by stamping onto the instep.

The stamp onto the instep can be used as a separate action.

BLOCK & PARRY

Self-defense is more efficient when it *prevents* blows than when it involves *exchange* of blows. Many assaultive actions begin with a reaching or punching action. Instead of allowing the action to be completed, avoid it, deflect it or block it.

Blocks and parries are methods of avoiding getting hit; they are similar actions with overlapping function. A block action implies that force is being countered with force, whereas parrying implies deflection of the oncoming blow. For practical self-defense the difference is not critical and I tend to use the words interchangeably.

Parrying is assertive, rather than counter-aggressive. Parrying stops the intended aggressive action, and it conveys the message that you are capable of defending yourself. It is a way of taking control.

If you can use the parry/block with moderate skill, you can handle many kinds of assault with the least possible use of strength or force.

31

SLAPPING PARRY

31. The partner who plays the role of assailant reaches out, first with one hand and then with the other. As he reaches out with his right hand, slap/parry cross-body with your open palm to divert and deflect the blow. It should be a snappy, vigorous action, not a pushing action.

As he reaches out with his left hand, slap the outside of his arm cross-body with your right hand. Practice the cross-body snap/parry until you are fairly comfortable doing it. The cross-body parry at the outside of his arm puts your assailant into an awkward position.

32

SLASHING PARRY

32. You can use open-handed slashing blows to parry high blows, as shown, or you can use them to parry low blows. Practice using the slash/parry against reaching or simulated punching high and low and against right and left blows.

33. You can use double-handed slashing parries if you are out to the side of the reaching arm.

34. If you block with your forearm, you must be closer in to your assailant than if you use the open-handed slash.

The parry actions are fundamental to efficient defense, even though they are not flashy or spectacular. Practice parrying and blocking right- and left-handed reaches. Practice stopping low reaching gestures, as though the intent were to grip your wrist. Stop reaches simulating intended cloth grab at your chest. Stop head-height reaches which simulate a gesture toward your face.

33

34

RESPONSE TO FRONT REACH

Many hostile or aggressive actions begin with a reaching arm. You do not have to wait until the aggressive action is completed; stop the arm before it touches you. You do not have to think about the specific intention. Your response would be the same if the adversary were trying to grab, poke, pull, shove or slap. Your response is to the reaching arm, not to a completed action.

As a practice procedure, take turns stopping the reaching arm with the various parries and blocking techniques.

35. Partners stand within normal distance, as though talking.

36. When the assailant partner starts to reach out, defending partner steps back and blocks.

35

36

                    37   38

BLOCKING THE FOUR QUARTERS

This is a practice procedure to develop block and parry
skills. It does not correspond to a realistic assault, but will
improve your general self-defense capability.

Begin practicing in slow motion. As your skill increases,
practice for quick reactions to the blows.

37. Partners stand just out of fist hitting range. At first,
the partner simulating the assailant should repeat a simple
sequence of two high blows, right . . .

38. . . . and left, followed by . . .

39   40

39. . . . two low blows, right and . . .

40. . . . left.

Practice this simple procedure a few times. Then without accelerating the speed of delivery, the assailant partner begins to mix his blows so that they do not follow any pattern. As partners develop the skill to respond quickly and appropriately, the practice procedure can become more and more complex and include feints and faking actions.

GESTURES OF ASSERTION

To convince a threatening, hostile individual that you will
not be a passive victim, your behavior must be totally believable. Your words and your body movements and your facial
expression must be convincing. Comparison between passive
and assertive behavior is illustrated here.

41. The man in this photo is threatening by his gesture and
his verbal message. The man on the left, though he is not
cowering down in fright, is in a passive stance. He appears
vulnerable.

42. He allows the intended aggressive act to be completed--
passive behavior.

43. The assertive response to the aggressive gesture . . .

44. . . . is to step back, hand raised in a guarding position.
This movement is accompanied by appropriate facial expression and a comment which indicates that you are not
looking for a fight, but can take care of yourself if necessary.

Don't mumble; speak clearly. Don't shout; speak loud enough
enough to be heard. Don't smile; maintain a serious expression. Maintain eye contact.

41

42

43

44

45   46

45, 46. Be prepared to use defense actions to stop the assault if necessary.

Partners should take turns playing the part of threatening and being threatened. It is essential preparation for being assertive. If you feel extremely uncomfortable when you behave assertively, it probably means that you need this role-playing practice and can benefit from it.

Partners can help each other by being very serious about this procedure. The threatening partner should make his threat believable by body gesture, tone of voice and facial expression. The partner who is rehearsing the assertive role must respond in a convincing manner; his body gesture, tone of voice and facial expression should convey the message, "Don't touch me!"

THE JOLLY BULLY

There are some acts which are not assaults, but which are, nonetheless, hostile.

Friends may engage in rough-and-tumble horsing around if they have equal status in these games. But when one person always plays the role of aggressor and the other person is always the butt of the game, the victim, though he might not be hurt physically, suffers embarrassment and shame.

Assertive behavior is ordinarily enough to stop this sort of abusive "play." The physical actions which might have to be used should be appropriate to the situation. Dealing with the jolly bully is not the same as coping with an assault where physical harm is intended. You need only make a convincing show of your determination to refuse to accept the abusive behavior in a passive manner.

If you have been subjected to humiliating horseplay over a long period of time you probably need the backup of knowing how to handle the bully if he does not respond to verbal commands. Practice the defense actions which follow, but realize that the foregoing material on gestures of assertion is just as important, if not more important, than the instruction on use of the physical actions.

The person who acts the role of friendly, jolly bully does it because he is allowed to get away with it. In most instances he will respond to assertive verbal commands to stop it and in many cases he will apologize for his offensive behavior.

47   48

THE HAND SQUEEZER

47. He is gripping your hand and does not respond to a verbal request to let go.

48. Extend your middle knuckle and grind into the top of his hand.

49   50

49. Or grip one of his fingers and lever it away.

50. Or using the bony edge of your forearm, grind into the bony part of his forearm.

If he is persistent and stubborn, you might slash onto the forearm and/or kick into the shin to complete the action.

51

52

53

THE LEANER

51. The leaner is always bigger than you are and he puts body weight behind this annoying action. Tell him to stop. Or duck down slightly and take a step back as you tell him to stop.

52. Or dig your extended knuckle into his side, just below the last rib.

53. Or grind your heel into the top of his instep.

54

55

THE SHOULDER PUNCHER/BACK SLAPPER

54. If he does not respond to your instruction to stop . . .

55. . . . you can slash his arm with as much vigor as needed to convince him that you are serious.

56

57

BEAR HUG

56. You are captured in a strong grip; he digs his chin into your backbone and digs his knuckles into your breast bone.

57. As you grip one of his fingers, kick into his shin . . .

58

59

58. . . . and scrape down his shinbone as you pull outward on his finger . . .

59. . . . to effect release.

60

61

62

BUTT GRIP

60. Dig into the back of his hand with your extended middle knuckle . . .

61. . . . and when you feel his grip loosen somewhat, wheel about with a snappy action, slashing his arm as you turn. This should effect release and in most instances would complete the defense.

62. If necessary, use a hand blow.

FIGHTING STANCES: PRO & CON AND AN ALTERNATIVE

Exotic-looking fighting stances have become commonplace
in movie and television fight scenes. Fighting stances have
almost no positive value outside of sport matches. In contest fighting stances are functional. In films the fighting
stances are used not for their practical value but for their
entertainment value.

Fighting stances, as a part of self-defense in the real world,
are of dubious psychological value much of the time, and
of limited tactical value.

There are some times when a fighting stance is useful for
handling threat of assault, but other times when a fighting
stance is neither appropriate nor desirable and might have
negative value. Against a back attack, a body grab, or a
mugging or choking assault, it is impossible to take a fighting
stance. It would be absurd to take a fighting stance in preparation for dealing with hostile behavior which is merely
annoying.

Responding to the threat of assault by taking a fighting
stance tells your adversary that he is calling the shots. If
you take a fighting stance, you relinquish the choice of
positive, non-aggressive control; you are committed to fighting if your adversary feels challenged by your stance.

Avoid the role of passive victim. Avoid the role of counter-
aggressor. Cowering down or showing fright is the passive
role. Taking a fighting stance is an aggressive role.

READY STANCES

If there is any possibility of avoiding physical action, you
can take a ready stance, which is neutral in gesture, permits
you to negotiate, and allows you to move quickly and de-
fensively if you must. Taking a ready stance is like putting
up an invisible guard. You have flexibility of response,
you are prepared to act, yet nothing about the way you are
standing or holding your hands indicates belligerence.

63

64

63. The natural-looking, thoughtful guard assumed by the man on the right does not suggest aggression or challenge. Realizing that a threat is developing, he takes a modified boxer's foot stance for strong balance, puts one hand up to his face and places the other hand under his arm.

64. From the ready position, he can move quickly, using a hand blow, or simply thrust his hand toward the adversary to startle and disconcert him.

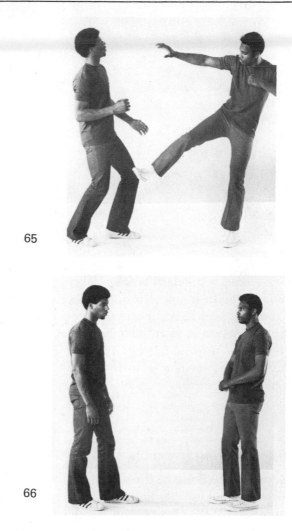

65

66

65. Or if the situation warrants it, he can quickly hit and kick.

66. Another ready stance is with both hands held in front of you. Your right hand is fisted and covered by your open left hand. Create a tension by pushing forward with your right hand as you pull back with your left. If necessary, you can move quickly, using a hand blow, or you can hit and kick from this position.

67

67. Taking a standard boxing fighting stance has a special advantage, for it gives the appearance of conventionality. From this stance, it appears that you will use the same style of action as he intends to use against you, adding the element of surprise to your defense. The boxing fighting stance is an excellent posture--it gives good guard and good balance and allows flexibility of hand and foot movement.

QUICK RESPONSE TO BACK THREAT

If you can respond to threat of assault from the back *before* the assault has been completed, you can cope much more efficiently. You should be able to deal with completed assaults, but it is easier to respond before the intended action is completed.

Practice procedure: Standing behind you, your partner touches you lightly on the shoulder. Turn quickly with one arm in a blocking position. Take turns doing this until you respond without hesitation.

Standing behind you, your partner moves his hand until you
can see it out of the corner of your eye. The moment you
see movement, turn around with one arm in blocking
position. Take turns doing this.

If you are in a quiet area, you can take turns giving each
other sound cues.

You are rehearsing the prudent response to the clues which
signal "danger behind you." You are safer if you turn to
face a possible threat than if you keep your back turned to it.

68

When you have practiced the turn-and-block gesture, pro-
ceed to practice responding to assault attempts such as
grabbing or choking from behind. Instead of giving a
slight cue, partners will now take turns attempting to complete a particular action. Use a variety of parry and block
actions as you practice.

68. For example, your partner starts the action of a finger
choke. Do not allow him to complete his intended action.

69

70

69. The instant you feel his hands touch you, wheel around sharply and block/slash his arm . . .

70. . . . and kick into the shin. Complete the defense with appropriate hand and foot blows.

DISTRACTION

Against a serious assault, distraction gives you a time-and-attention advantage over your assailant. Distraction can be thrusting hand movements, yelling, throwing an object toward the assailant's face, or rapid foot movement.

Except in the instance where you would *not* want to startle your assailant, such as close-in knife threat, loud yelling, rapid movements or a thrown object will disconcert, disorient, and confuse him. Even when the thrown object cannot hurt him, it is distracting.

Distraction can divert an intended assault and give you time to move out of range; it can give you a few seconds of time in which to put yourself in good guard, ready to hit and kick.

Whenever an intended victim behaves in an unexpected manner, it disrupts the planned action of the assailant.

FEINTING DISTRACTIONS

Feinting actions are excellent tactical moves for self-defense. Feinting is a diversion; the assailant reacts to your feint or fake, giving you a chance to start your planned defense.

71. A sudden arm movement upward can get his attention for an instant.

71

72

72. Or a quick thrusting hand movement toward his face makes him draw back . . .

73

73. . . . and you complete your defense with kicks or other defense actions.

SPIN-AROUNDS

If you can get around behind your assailant, you are less
vulnerable to his intended assault. You can push him away,
apply a simple takedown, or escape more easily.

Practice the spin-arounds in conjunction with a blocking or
parrying action.

74

75

ARM SPIN-AROUND

74. Slash or block the reaching or hitting arm . . .

75. . . . and grip it with the same hand you use for blocking.
Using his forward movement to help your action, pull him
forward, and then . . .

76, 77. . . . sharply around so that you are behind him and can complete your defense with appropriate hand and foot blows, or a takedown.

76   77

78   79

BODY SPIN-AROUND

78, 79. Block or slash at your partner's reaching arms, and without hesitation begin the spin-around by thrusting at his left shoulder with your right hand as you push at the back of his right shoulder with your left hand, using a snappy action . . .

80

80. . . . to turn him counterclockwise, in position for a takedown, or other suitable ending.

Practice the spin-around counterclockwise and clockwise to determine which seems more comfortable for you.

JUDO THROWS

It is thrilling to watch spectacular throwing in movie fight scenes; it is exciting to watch sport judo matches in which the throwing techniques are executed in a display of seemingly effortless style.

For practical defense, the throwing techniques are not feasible. The high degree of technical skill needed to achieve throwing ability and the constant, ongoing practice needed to maintain this skill are factors which eliminate judo throws for basic self-defense.

There are many modern assault situations in which a judo throw would not be possible and many situations in which a judo throw would be inappropriately violent.

TAKEDOWNS

Sometimes putting an assailant onto the ground gives you
a time advantage--extra seconds in which to make your
escape. Sometimes it is necessary for psychological reasons
to put an assailant onto the ground to signal that the assault
has ended.

The takedowns which follow are simple, practical methods
of putting an assailant onto the ground.

81   82

FOREWARD TAKEDOWN

81. An efficient action is one which takes advantage of
your assailant's movement. You have positioned yourself
behind the assailant and kicked into the back of his knee.
As he loses his balance forward . . .

82. . . . push him in the direction he is moving to put him
on the ground.

83   84

BACK TAKEDOWN

83. Simulate hand and foot blows and then wheel your
partner around so that you are behind him, out to the side
(not directly in back of him). Grip his shoulder or hair with
one hand and place your foot into the back of his knee.

For safety in practice, support your partner with your
other hand.

As you pull back with your arms, push with your foot. If
your partner stands in a normal stance, you will see how
little effort is needed to pull him back off balance. If
you used a vigorous kick into the back of his knee as you
pulled back sharply with your hand, he would go to the
ground.

84. It is not necessary to complete the action down to the
ground, but if your partner loses his balance ease him down
by maintaining your hand grips.

Avoid positioning yourself directly behind your partner.
You should not be in the line of his fall. Avoid being pulled
down as he goes down.

HOLDS & LOCKS FOR RESTRAINT

It is more prudent to get away from an assailant than it is
to attempt to apply a restraining hold. The lay citizen does
not have the same duty as the professional who must arrest
or keep an individual in custody.

Nevertheless there are times when it might be necessary to
restrain an aggressive person. If there is a potentially violent
(or self-destructive) person you might have to cope with, it
would be useful to know how to restrain. The techniques
which follow are relatively simple to learn and easy to apply.

BASIC ARM BAR

85. Your partner, shown right, extends his right arm. You
grip his wrist with your right hand.

86. Pulling his captured arm forward and twisting it clockwise, you step around to place yourself at his side . . .

87. . . . and press down onto the back of his elbow with
your left forearm.

This technique can be applied as a walk-along using moderate
force. You can step along briskly as you maintain the wrist
twist and the pressure onto his elbow. Or if appropriate,
it can be applied forcefully to put an assailant onto the
ground; instead of pressing down with your forearm, you
would apply a smashing forearm blow.

85

86

87

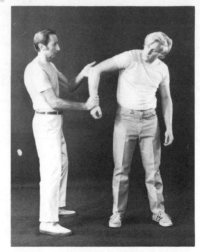

88   89

REAR BENT-ARM LOCK

88. Grip your partner's right wrist with your right hand.

89. Hit at the outside of his elbow with your left hand to
bend his arm, as shown . . .

90   91

90. . . . and step around behind him as you twist his captured arm back and up. From this position you can place your left hand at his shoulder and push him forward as you continue the upward pressure on his wrist . . .

91. . . . or you can grip hair and continue pressure on his captured wrist as you walk him forward.

COMPLETE DEFENSES

The two concepts fundamental to this method of self-defense are: flexible combinations of basic actions and on-going defense.

Both of these concepts go counter to the old-style karate, jujitsu and aikido methods, which rely on rigid series of "moves" in which a specific defense is a reaction to a specific attack.

ON-GOING DEFENSE

Most defenses are completed with very few actions--just enough to demonstrate a refusal to play the part of helpless victim. The number of actions will vary with the situation. The concept of on-going defense can be applied if you use one action or if you use several in combination. If only one technique comes to mind, use it over and over as required to complete the defense. If you use a combination, continue the defense actions until you have stopped the assault.

FLEXIBLE COMBINATIONS

Repeating one or two defense techniques as required makes an on-going defense. Combining three or four techniques in a flexible manner and repeating them as necessary makes a more sophisticated, effective defense. The ability to use the basic material in a flexible way eliminates the need to recall a specific series of "moves" and frees you from the rigid pattern of action-reaction. The concepts of on-going and flexible are more realistic than the set-pattern defenses. You cannot depend on an assailant to perform a set pattern of assault moves to which you respond in a set pattern of defense moves.

Remember that you are practicing concepts. Begin practice of both concepts in slow motion. Practice partners take turns, and the partner playing the role of assailant acts as a reference target only. As you gain assurance and experience in practicing the on-going combinations, you can speed up the actions and the partner playing the role of assailant can provide reaction moves to which you respond in an appropriate manner.

Try to avoid getting into the habit of repeating the same series of actions. You might develop a favored sequence, which is fine, but do not rely on set, rigid patterns.

Observe the safety rules carefully. In this, as in any of the other practice procedures, you need not hurt each other to gain the objective of the practice.

The combinations which are illustrated are examples and are intended to get you started. After you practice the example combinations, make up your own combinations.

If you know ten actions and use only four of those ten in any possible combination, you can make more than five thousand different combinations.

COMPLETE COMBINATIONS

First, practice the combinations illustrated. Work for smooth, rhythmical, on-going actions.

92. Block high . . .

93. . . . block low . . .

92   93

94   95

94, 95. . . . kick, hit . . .

96, 97. . . .spin-around, ready for a takedown.

Finally, the objective of combination practice is to gain the
ability to make *any* appropriate combination of defense
tactics appropriate to the situation.

Your first attempts at making your own combinations will
take some time and thinking. Do your thinking before you
practice. Thinking about what you might do is your mental
rehearsal. At first, you will have to plan your combinations.
Partners help each other by pointing out ways of improving
the combinations. Make your suggestions in a positive manner. For instance, if your partner consistently fails to use
both of his hands for hand blows, tell him to use his left
hand (or right hand) more. In general, if you tell him what
to do, rather than what he has done wrong, you encourage
and help, rather than criticize and discourage.

96 97

YELLING AS A DEFENSE AID

A sudden, loud, unexpected yell is startling and disconcerting. It can be used with your other actions to increase the effectiveness of your defense.

The usual reaction to a sudden noise is fear and disorientation. All the symptoms of fright--faster heart beat, trembling hands, accelerated breathing--can be induced by yelling at your opponent. Even if the disorientation period is very short, it will help you in your defense.

Yelling is an outward show of courage which has a psychological effect on your adversary. Whether or not you feel an inner courage, if you behave in a brave and determined manner, your assailant will perceive you as brave. Bullies do not look for brave adversaries; they want passive victims.

The act of yelling gives impact and a surge of extra power to your physical actions. Like the grunt which automatically accompanies lifting or pushing a heavy object, the yell tightens your abdomen and helps concentrate energy for most efficient self-defense.

98

99

FULL-NELSON RELEASE

98. You are held in a full nelson.

99. Relieve pain and pressure by putting your clasped hands at your own forehead and pushing back.

100. Kick vigorously into his shin until you feel his grip relax somewhat.

101. When you feel his grip weakened, thrust your arms out and down, with a sharp, quick motion to break his grip . . .

102. . . . and turn around to face your assailant, ready to complete your defense with hand . . .

103. . . . and foot blows, if necessary, to complete your defense.

100

101

102

103

104   105

HEADLOCK RELEASES

Release I.

104. You are captured in a front headlock, as shown. Grip his arm at the wrist and just below the elbow to relieve the pain and pressure.

105. Maintaining your hold, kick into his shin.

106. Repeat the kicks until you feel his grip relax somewhat. With a vigorous, jerky motion thrust his arms away . . .

107. . . . as you back out from under his grip and kick, if necessary, to complete your defense.

Release II

108. You are captured in a headlock, as shown. Grip his arm with both hands, one at his wrist and one just below his elbow. Pull down to counteract his grip. Kick with vigor into his shin until you feel his grip relax somewhat.

106   107

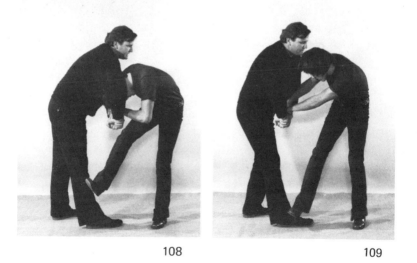

108   109

109. When his grip is weakened, thrust down sharply with your arms to effect release.

FOREARM CHOKE: MUGGING DEFENSE

110. The defending partner is pulled back off balance by
a forearm choke. Partner who applies the choke must note:
Take a firm grip on your partner by clamping your hand
onto his *shoulder* and placing your other hand over it to
secure your grip. Apply *very light pressure* at his throat,
just enough to simulate the gesture of the assault.

111. Defending partner: Tap for immediate release if your
partner applies painful pressure at your throat. Grip the
choking forearm with both your hands, at his wrist and
just below his elbow. Pull down on his arm, putting all of
your body weight into the action.

Turn your head into the bend of his elbow to reduce choking
pressure. If you do not relieve the pressure at your throat,
you are in danger of losing consciousness.

If you try to defend by using hand or arm blows, you are
vulnerable to the choking pressure. If you struggle to stand
upright, you *increase* the choking pressure. You must reduce
the choking pressure before you do anything else!

Maintaining the firm grip on his arm, kick forcefully into his
shin with the edge of your shoe; scrape down along his shin
and stamp onto his instep. Repeat the kick-scrape-stamp
until you feel his grip relax slightly.

Simulate these actions with spirit. Assailant partner, react
as though you had been kicked and stamped.

112. When his grip is slightly loosened, maintaining your
firm grip on his arm, *back out* from under his arm . . .

113. . . . using one or two additional kicks or stamps, if
necessary, to aid your escape . . .

110

111

112

113

114   115

114. . . . and when you are free, continue to step around
behind him, still gripping his arm . . . which you can pull up
behind him . . . or you can push him away . . .

115. . . . or you can complete the defense by kicking into
the back of his knee for a take-down ending.

DEFENSE AGAINST KICKING ASSAULTS

Toe Kick

116. A counter-kick into the shin blocks a toe kick. Finish with hand blows or any appropriate action.

116

Knee Kick   117   118

117. The knee kick is a forceful blow which is difficult to counter, but relatively easy to parry. As you side-step to move out of the direct line of his attack, slap-parry his knee vigorously, using a one-handed or two-handed parry . . .

118. . . . to deflect the blow and turn his body. Because he is on one-point balance, you could move him around so that he has his back to you. Complete your defense with a kick into the back of his knee or any other appropriate action.

119. Parry a high stamp-
ing kick in the same man-
ner. Complete the defense
by kicking into the back of
the knee, if necessary.

119

120

120. You are on the ground and your adversary tries to
kick. Put your body weight onto your hands so that you can
swivel freely on your buttocks. Kick at his shins. Don't let
him get around near your head.

In practice, the partner playing the role of assailant must be
very careful not to come within range of the defending
partner's kicks. The object is to avoid letting the adversary
get into position where he could kick at the head or into
the side of the defending partner. As he attempts to move
around to avoid the kicking action, the defending partner
swivels to follow his movement and continues kicking.

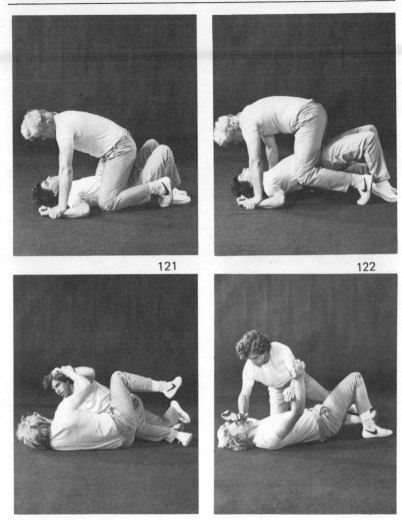

PIN ESCAPE   123   124

121,122. You are pinned. Draw your feet up close to your buttocks.

123. With a sudden, lunging action, bridge up with your feet and your buttocks. If you are considerably smaller than your assailant, you will not be able to bridge to the extent shown in the photo, but you can bridge enough to make the next action effective.

124. Thrust one leg forward and wheel your body in the direction of the extended leg, using your braced, bent leg to help push him over and off, allowing you to escape. Back away from him and rise when you are out of reach of his arms and legs, or use hand blows to complete your defense before rising.

125   126

RIGID WEAPON ASSAULTS

The most effective defense against a rigid hitting object*
involves moving in to stay out of range of the weapon.
This is one of the very few instances in which a defense is
safe close in. You would not move close in to defend if
you could escape without resorting to physical action.

The two most common ways of using a stick weapon are
the outside swing and the back-handed swing. The defenses
are similar.

OUTSIDE SWING

125. The gesture of the outside swing is very broad--there
is no mistaking the style of the assault. As the attack begins,
move in close and block his hitting arm--*not* the weapon--
with both your arms. The forearm block, shown, is effective; you could also use slashing open-handed blocks . . .

126. . . . and, without hesitation, grip his arm with both
your hands, extending your arms rigidly to immobilize his
arm briefly. Kick into his leg. Complete the defense with
hand and foot blows as needed.

*Examples are a chair, shovel, pool cue, lug wrench or
similar implements.

127   128

BACK-HANDED SWING

127. The stick (or similar weapon) is held cross-body, ready to swing back. Step in and to the outside of the hitting arm and block the arm--*not* the weapon--with both your arms, using your fists, as shown, or double slashing blocks . . .

128. . . . or double forearm blocks . . . and immediately grip his arm with both your hands and extend your arms rigidly to immobilize his arm for the brief time necessary to complete your defense with vigorous kicks.

Practice the defense against the two kinds of assaults, first as separate actions, and then practice them as a combination in which the assailant misses at his first attempt because you step *back* to avoid the first swing and then step *in* to defend against his second swing.

If your partner swings back-handed the first time, step back to avoid it and be ready to step in for the defense as he begins his outside swing. If your partner swings outside at the first attempt, step *back* to avoid it and then step *in* to defend against the back-handed action. Be very careful with your partner to avoid getting hit. It is safest to work with a padded stick.

FLEXIBLE WEAPONS

A flexible weapon, such as a chain or belt, is used with the same kinds of gestures as the back-handed and outside-swinging stick attacks, but the movement of the weapon is such that the defense can be made *only* when the weapon is in the back-handed swinging position.

129. If you attempt to move in close while the chain is swinging wide, it will hit you as you make your defense. Watch for the assault to begin and step or leap back as it comes toward you and . . .

129

130

130. . . . as it clears you and before he can start the reaction swing, move in . . .

131. . . . and block his arm, with both your hands . . .

132. . . . and grip his arm. Extend your arms rigidly to immobilize his arm for the brief time required for completing the defense with kicks, as necessary.

131

132

YOKING ARM PIN RELEASE

This situation would not be serious unless you were being held by one assailant so that a second individual could threaten assault.

If no other assailant were involved, release might be effected by kicking into the shin and then twisting around sharply to free one arm. As illustrated, a second assailant is implied.

133. Your arms are pinned and you are being threatened by a second assailant (not shown). The man holding you is not hurting you; he is restraining you. You can use him for support.

134. Kick vigorously into the legs of the front assailant, continuing as necessary to hurt him enough to make him back off.

135. When you have driven the front assailant away, kick into the shins of the man holding you, and . . .

136. . . . scrape down with the edge of your shoe . . . and stamp onto his instep. Repeat this action as necessary until you feel his grip somewhat relaxed.

133

134

135

136

137. Then twist your body sharply around to one side.
This action will result in one arm becoming more firmly
pinned, but it will loosen his grip on your other arm. Try
this action alone with your practice partner and you will
feel that the free arm is the one on the side to which you
turn. In the photo, the defending partner is twisting toward
his right side and it is, accordingly, his right arm which is
more free.

138. With a rapid, thrusting action, pull the free arm upward, hitting up with your elbow.

139. When you have released one arm, spin out in the
opposite direction to free your other arm. Hit and kick as
necessary.

137

138

139

KNIFE ASSAULT DEFENSES

If a knife or other weapon is used for intimidation, and the
primary intent is robbery, not assault, do NOT attempt a
defense. It is reckless and foolish to risk injury to protect
property or money. *Any* defense against a knife assault
involves some risk of being cut, though the defense shown
involves the least danger of injury.

If you feel that being cooperative and quiet will prevent
the assault, the prudent action is quiet cooperation. If
the only two choices you have are passive submission to
being knifed or making a defense, make a spirited defense.

Grappling with or gripping the knife or trying to disarm
the assailant is dangerous. The traditional aikido or jujitsu
defense against knife assault is very difficult. The most
efficient defense is that which deflects the intended assault
without making you vulnerable to the most serious cutting
actions.

CLOSE-IN KNIFE THREAT

With sufficient attention to the preventive procedures of
defense, you should be able to avoid being cornered in this
manner. If you know how to cope with this kind of threat,
you should be able to deal with it in a more prudent, calm
manner, thus minimizing the danger. The knife-armed
assailant expects his intended victim to betray helplessness
and panic. Individuals have calmly talked their way out of
frightening situations. DO NOT ATTEMPT A DEFENSE
if the knife is being used as intimidation only.

140   141

140. The knife is held close. Put your hands up immediately and talk to the assailant. Tell him you do not intend to oppose him if he is not going to hurt you. Speak quietly and make eye contact.

141. If you judge that he is going to cut you if you do not attempt a defense, start with a *subtle*, slight eye or hand motion to briefly distract his attention. Before doing this, you have noted which hand holds the knife because you are going to thrust his knife-holding hand cross-body.

142   143

142. Parry his knife-holding hand cross-body with a vigorous, snappy action as you thrust your hand toward his
face. In practice with your partner, simulate the thrusting
action, but be very careful not to make contact with his
eyes! In actual defense against a knife-wielding assailant,
you would be justified in using eye-stabs as part of your
defense.

143. Grip his arm with both your hands and stiffen your
arms to immobilize his knife hand for the brief time needed
to complete your defense with vigorous, forceful kicks into
his knee.

Do not attempt to wrest the knife away unless you are
certain he is not going to struggle. If you have hurt him or
put him on the ground, you might be able to disarm him
without danger to yourself, but if you can escape without
disarming him, do it!

AFTERWORD

For basic, practical self-defense it is best to know a small group of techniques which you can use in flexible combinations and which you can remember without difficulty.

If, after practicing the defenses in this book, you do not feel confident of your ability to use the material, repeat the course. It would only intensify your problem to add additional material or more complicated techniques.

When you have become moderately adept, an occasional run-through of the defense actions and some occasional mental practice should help to keep your proficiency at a functional level.

Mental practice does not mean that you brood or worry about the possibility of assault; it means mental review of possible responses to common types of assault. When you have prepared yourself to cope with the emergency of assault, you do not have to worry about it as much as when you felt inadequate to deal with the situation.

FURTHER STUDY

If you wish to develop more than functional skill in self-defense or if you wish to practice for a physical fitness program, or if you have become interested in a specific specialty of weaponless fighting, you can do further work at home, you might wish to join a class, or you might be interested in organizing a group to practice with you.

Most of the people who are interested in self-defense and related fighting skills do not have access to personal instruction. Only those who live in certain areas have any choice of schools or teachers. Some "Y"s and civic recreation centers offer classes in judo, karate and aikido for sport and physical fitness. Some physical education departments offer basic self-defense in secondary schools.

CHOOSING A SCHOOL

If you live in a community which has a school, observe a
class in session and then you can decide whether or not the
teacher suits you. If there is more than one school, visit
them and compare. You are the best judge of what is best
for you even though you do not have a technical back-
ground. You are equipped with a more important gauge
for making a decision--your own reaction to what you see!

Any reliable school or teacher will allow you to observe
at least one complete session before you make up your
mind. Verbal explanations of what is being taught are not
enough; you have to see what it is. Nor should you allow
yourself to be dazzled by what the teacher can do. You are
not paying to see him perform; you are paying him for what
he can teach *you* to do.

When you observe a class, watch the teacher and watch the
students. Does the teacher actually instruct? Does he
give clear directions and explain what is to be done, or
does he merely demonstrate and leave the students to imitate
as well as they can? Is the teacher patient and does he encourage the students, or is he cross and rude to students who
need correction or help?

Do the students seem enthusiastic about what they are
doing? Do they appear to be helpful to one another? Is
there a friendly atmosphere?

Is the material being practiced what you think *you* would
like to learn?

If you like what you see, the school is right for you. If
you don't like what you see, the school is not right for
you, even though the teacher, the material and the method
might be quite acceptable to other individuals.

DON'T SIGN A CONTRACT unless you are absolutely certain that you understand what you are signing and that it is a fair contract. Unless you are familiar with contracts, you may need help in deciding whether or not the contract protects your consumer rights. If you sign a contract without reading or understanding it, you may find yourself obligated to pay for lessons you don't want to take or you may find that you cannot get a refund in case of emergency.

As a general rule, you are better protected if you make partial payments as you go along than if you pay for a full course in advance. If you make partial payments and then change your mind or lose interest or move, you are not tied to an arrangement which might be a financial burden.

If you need help in deciding if a contract is fair, if a financial arrangement is fair, or if the operator of a school is reliable, ask your local Chamber of Commerce or your librarian to direct you. Most communities have agencies which offer free advice and guidance in these matters.

It is your money and your time which are being spent. You have the right to spend them the way you please and to make sure that you will get your money's worth.

DOES TEACHER NEED A BLACK BELT?

It is a common misconception that only a black belt holder can teach self-defense and related fighting skills.

A black belt indicates a high degree of achievement. Much time and effort go into that achievement. But it does not necessarily follow that a black belt holder is a competent teacher. Most black belts are awarded for excellence in contest. The qualities which make a tournament champion are not those which make an outstanding teacher.

In every type of activity which requires physical training you
will find examples of good teachers who are not necessarily
good performers and you will find excellent performers who
are not skilled teachers. This field is no different. Physical
education teachers are proving this point dramatically.
Throughout the United States, many physical education
teachers, men and women, are teaching successful classes
of basic self-defense in secondary schools. Although they
have not had previous experience in this specialty and
though they do not have belt degrees, they are particularly
well-suited to the instruction of basic self-defense because
they are teachers.

Physical directors of recreation centers are also teaching
basic self-defense with good results. Such teachers understand community needs, they are sensitive to the fact that
defenses must be modern, safe and ethical, and they do
not confuse the modern urban community with the settings
of Samurai warrior movies.

COLORED BELTS

The ancient forms of weaponless fighting did not award
belt degrees, wear special uniforms or engage in contest.
Judo was the first of the Asian specialties of hand-to-hand
combat to be modified and adapted for modern sport with
the objective of physical development. With its conversion
to sport and physical education uses, judo players were
ranked according to skill in competition and demonstration
of formal technique. Contrary to popular belief, the first
black belt holders were not deadly killers; they were skilled
sportsmen.

The myth of the black belt has spread widely and many
people are convinced that the wearer of a black belt has
superhuman powers, that only a black belt qualifies a
teacher of self-defense, that one must have a colored belt
to validate self-defense skills, and so on through a long list
of erroneous information about belt ranking.

The colored belts of judo, karate and other weaponless fighting are awarded primarily for contest skill or for performance of rehearsed routines. Since no school or style of any of the fighting skills awards belts in the same manner and since no school or style acknowledges the validity of a colored belt earned in any other school or style, the colored belt ranks have significance only in the school or system in which they are awarded.

Self-defense can be learned without ranks or colored belts. The requirement of working toward belt ranks as a prerequisite for learning basic self-defense, is, in my view, an impediment to teaching and learning practical self-defense.

Because many of my students expressed a desire to go beyond basic techniques of self-defense and wanted to continue practicing for physical fitness and recreation, I devised a system called JUKADO.* Jukado combines self-defense and fitness exercises and includes a method of grading proficiency by colored belt ranks. But I must emphasize that colored belts need not be a factor in learning the fundamentals of self-defense.

* *Bruce Tegner's Complete Book of Jukado*
Thor Publishing Company, Ventura, CA 93001

INDEX

arm bar/76
assertiveness/14, 18, 52
avoidance/21
back threat, response to/66
belt ranking/107
bent-arm lock/78
blocking/44
   practice procedure/50
body image/17
bully/55
colored belts/107, 108
combining defense actions
   complete/81
   flexible/80
conditioning hands/26
defense
   complete/80
   on-going/80
defenses against
   back slapping/59
   bear hug/60
   butt grip/62
   flexible weapons/96
   forearm choke/88
   full-nelson/84
   grabbing/48
   hand squeeze/56
   headlock/86
   kicking/91
   knife assault/102
   leaner/58
   mugging/88
   pin, ground/93
   pulling/48
   punching/39, 45, 47, 50, 59
   shoving/48
   stick weapons/94
   two assailants/98
   yoking arm pin/98

distraction/69
effects of blows/33
feinting/69
fight scenes, filmed/20
guns/19
hand blows
  boxing/36
  chop/27
  clawing/34
  edge-of-hand/27
  elbow/37
  fist/36
  hammer/35
  heel-of-palm/34
  karate punch/36
  poking/34
hand conditioning/26
hitchhiking/21
holds & locks/76, 78
judo throws/73
kicking, self-defense/37
kicks
  practical/40
  snap/43
  stamp/45
masculine myth/13
mental practice/105
parrying/44
  slapping/45
  slashing/46
passivity/16
practice procedures/23, 25
reaching, response to/48
restraints/76, 78
safety in practice/23, 25, 35, 42, 88
school, selection of/106
self-esteem/17, 18
skill level/12
spin-arounds
  arm/71
  body/72

sport vs. self-defense/16, 40
stances
  boxing/66
  fighting/63
  ready/63
surprise, element of/22
takedowns/74
  back/75
  forward/74
tapping safety signal/24, 88
targets/31, 35
two assailants/98
yelling/83

BRUCE TEGNER books are on sale at bookstores and magazine stands throughout the world. If your local dealer does not stock the titles you want, you may order directly from the publisher.

For a free descriptive brochure, write to:

THOR PUBLISHING CO.
P.O. BOX 1782
VENTURA, CA 93001

BIFOCAL

A simple man believes every word he hears.
A clever man understands the need for proof.
—PROVERBS 14.15, *New English Bible*